# Three-Year Mom Journal

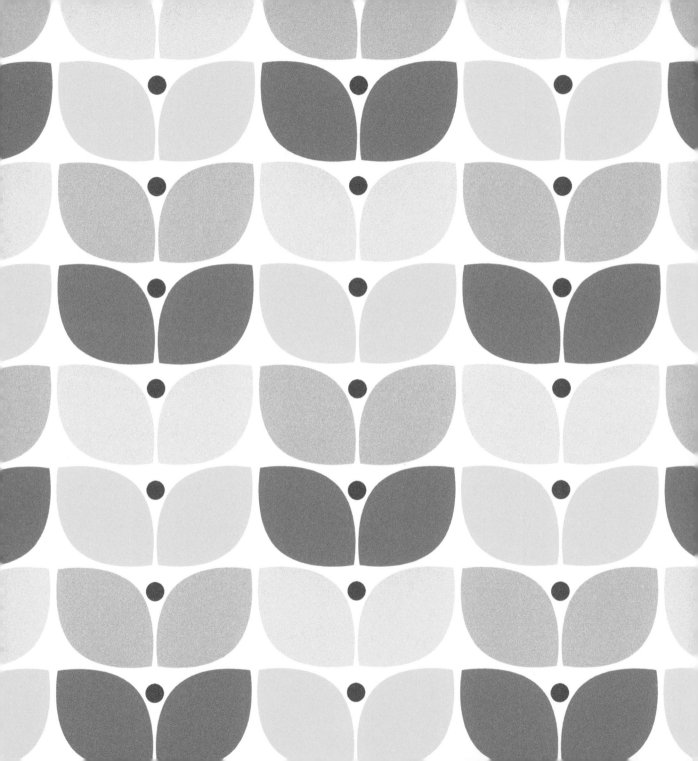

# Three-Year
# MOM
# JOURNAL

## One Question a Day to Prompt Reflection and Record Memories

SCARLET PAOLICCHI

ROCKRIDGE
PRESS

For general information on our other products and services or to obtain technical support, please contact our Customer Care Department within the United States at (866) 744-2665, or outside the United States at (510) 253-0500.

Rockridge Press publishes its books in a variety of electronic and print formats. Some content that appears in print may not be available in electronic books, and vice versa.

Cover Designer: Julie Schrader
Interior Designer: Lindsey Dekker
Art Producer: Hannah Dickerson
Editor: Adrian Potts
Production Editor: Rachel Taenzler
Production Manager: Holly Haydash

All illustrations used under license from Shutterstock.com and iStock.com.

Hardcover ISBN: 978-1-63878-650-4
Paperback ISBN: 978-1-63807-057-3
R0

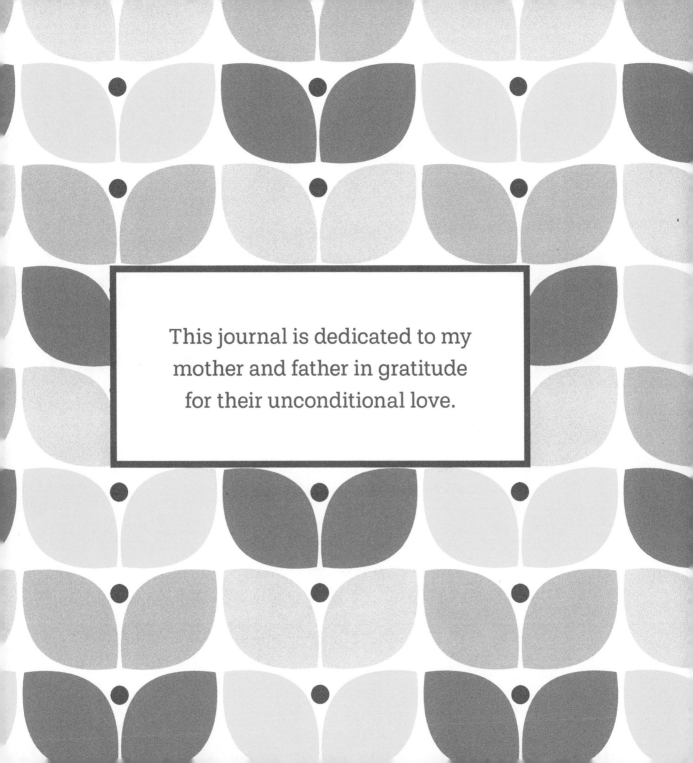

This journal is dedicated to my
mother and father in gratitude
for their unconditional love.

This journal belongs to

_____

# How to Use This Journal

**A**s a mother myself, I recognize what an amazing journey mother-hood is, and I am so grateful for it. Now that my kids are teenagers, I also know firsthand just how fast time flies! That is why I am so excited to share this journal with you, to help you keep a record of the special moments along the way.

This book is written to help you record observations, reflections, and memories about motherhood over the course of three years. You can write in it for three consecutive years, but if you end up skipping a year or two, you can still pick it up again whenever it's convenient. It will be fun to compare your answers over time as your kid(s) grows and changes so much from year to year! If there has not been a radical change in your answer to a particular question, that's a great opportunity to expand on the information or write about something different.

Each question in this journal is posed on a specific date. This is to help keep you on track with a manageable prompt for each day. However, don't feel pressured to answer one every single day—you can always catch up!

This journal is the perfect place to share everything from funny quotes your child(ren) has said to your heart's feelings on the joys and challenges of mother-hood. I have tried to offer a range of questions to keep things fun, fresh, and varied. Some are lighthearted, while others are designed to prompt deeper reflection.

Most questions are designed to be quick and easy to fill out with short answers. Others will elicit slightly longer responses. The final question of each month will provide an opportunity to share more in-depth stories or introspections. However, you shouldn't feel pressured to fill up all the space provided. Share as much or as little as you like.

The journal questions are divided into five categories to help provide structure and variety. These categories are interspersed throughout the book, and each will correspond to a particular icon for clear organization.

## This Past Year

These questions are for reflecting on things that happened during the past year—from the small details of life to big-picture changes.

## Looking Ahead

Here you will explore the dreams, hopes, and goals you have for the coming year and the future in general—both for yourself and for your family.

## On Motherhood

These questions are for charting your thoughts, feelings, and experiences about being a mother—including the surprising moments, the day-to-day challenges, and the greatest rewards.

## All About Your Child(ren)

Here you can reflect on and record all the memories and moments—both big and small—about your child(ren) as they grow.

## Just for Fun

These questions will help you recall and write about the funny events of everyday life and reveal a less serious side of yourself.

I hope you enjoy the process of writing in this journal and the opportunity to reflect on the experience of motherhood and capture its joys and challenges. This journal will also make a wonderful gift for your child(ren) someday—possibly when they become parents themselves. They will be sure to enjoy reading about the details of their childhood through the special light of your eyes.

## January 1
What is your New Year's resolution and why did you pick it? Share your child(ren)'s resolution(s) as well, if they have any.

20 _____

_____

_____

20 _____

_____

_____

20 _____

_____

_____


## January 2
What does your child(ren) do on a typical weekday?

20 _____

_____

_____

20 _____

_____

_____

20 _____

_____

_____

## January 3 — When did you most feel like a mom this past year?

**20** ___

**20** ___

**20** ___

## January 4 — What one word or phrase would you use to characterize the past year and why?

**20** ___

**20** ___

**20** ___

## January 5
If you and your child(ren) were to switch places for a day, what would you do?

20 _____
_____
_____

20 _____
_____
_____

20 _____
_____
_____

## January 6
How did things change most for your family over this past year?

20 _____
_____
_____

20 _____
_____
_____

20 _____
_____
_____

## January 7
What does your child(ren) do on a typical weekend? Is there a regular routine that you follow, or is it mostly free time? What are their favorite weekend activities? Who do they spend their time with?

**20**

**20**

**20**

## January 8
Write about something precious to you about your family's culture that you want to pass on to your child(ren). How will you accomplish this?

**20** _____

_____

_____

_____

_____

_____

_____

**20** _____

_____

_____

_____

_____

_____

_____

**20** _____

_____

_____

_____

_____

_____

_____

**January 9** What does your child(ren) do right now that you will miss as they grow and change over the coming year?

20 _____

20 _____

20 _____

**January 10** What animal does your child(ren) remind you of and why?

20 _____

20 _____

20 _____

## January 11
What was your favorite family vacation from this past year and why?

20 ___

20 ___

20 ___

## January 12
What are your child(ren)'s favorite foods?

20 ___

20 ___

20 ___

## January 13
What is your favorite duty each day as a mom? Share details about what you do and why you enjoy doing it.

20 _____

_____
_____
_____
_____
_____

20 _____

_____
_____
_____
_____
_____

20 _____

_____
_____
_____
_____
_____

## January 14

What are some of your aspirations for your next year as a mother?

**20** _____

_____

_____

_____

_____

_____

_____

**20** _____

_____

_____

_____

_____

_____

_____

**20** _____

_____

_____

_____

_____

_____

_____

## January 15
What silly thing do you do to make your child(ren) laugh?

20 _____

20 _____

20 _____

## January 16
What were some big family events that happened during the past year?

20 _____

20 _____

20 _____

## January 17
What aspect of your cultural heritage does your child(ren) enjoy most?

20 _____

20 _____

20 _____

## January 18
What is your least favorite duty each day as a mom? What about it don't you like?

20 _____

20 _____

20 _____

## January 19

What are some of the coming milestones for your child(ren) in the next year, and what excites you about them?

**20**____

_____

_____

_____

_____

_____

**20**____

_____

_____

_____

_____

_____

**20**____

_____

_____

_____

_____

_____

## January 20

If you could do anything in the world with your child(ren) today, what would it be and why?

**20** _____

_____

_____

_____

_____

_____

_____

**20** _____

_____

_____

_____

_____

_____

_____

**20** _____

_____

_____

_____

_____

_____

_____

## January 21

What were some big world-news headlines from this past year?

20 _____

20 _____

20 _____

## January 22

What is your child(ren)'s favorite thing to do?

20 _____

20 _____

20 _____

## January 23 — What does being a mom feel like?

20 _____

20 _____

20 _____

## January 24 — What's a favorite joke you have told your child(ren) recently or they have told you?

20 _____

20 _____

20 _____

## January 25

What is something that you would like to get better at as a family? How do you think you can work together to address this challenge or meet this goal?

**20**

**20**

**20**

## January 26

What was your favorite holiday celebration from this past year? Did you start or repeat any traditions? Do you have any stories to record about how your child(ren) was involved in the holiday or thoughts they shared about it?

**20**

**20**

**20**

## January 27
What is your child(ren)'s favorite toy? Describe it and write about why it is special to them.

20 _____

20 _____

20 _____

## January 28
What's one mundane fact you never knew about motherhood before you became a mom? It can be anything—for example, a detail about childbirth or breastfeeding.

20 _____

20 _____

20 _____

## January 29
What is something your family does that you are grateful for and want to keep doing as the year progresses?

20 _____

20 _____

20 _____

## January 30
What music do you play when you want to dance or have fun with your kid(s)?

20 _____

20 _____

20 _____

## January 31

What was one of your favorite days from this last year? Write down everything about it, even the little things, because the clarity of the memories is best captured in the details. Share why that day was special to you.

**20** ___

**20** ___

20

## February 1
What has changed most for your child(ren) this past year?

20 _____

20 _____

20 _____

## February 2
Does your child(ren) have a special source of comfort, like a blanket or a stuffed animal?

20 _____

20 _____

20 _____

### February 3
What emotions about becoming a mother have surprised you most?

20 _____

20 _____

20 _____

### February 4
Is there something new that you would like to try doing as a family this year?

20 _____

20 _____

20 _____

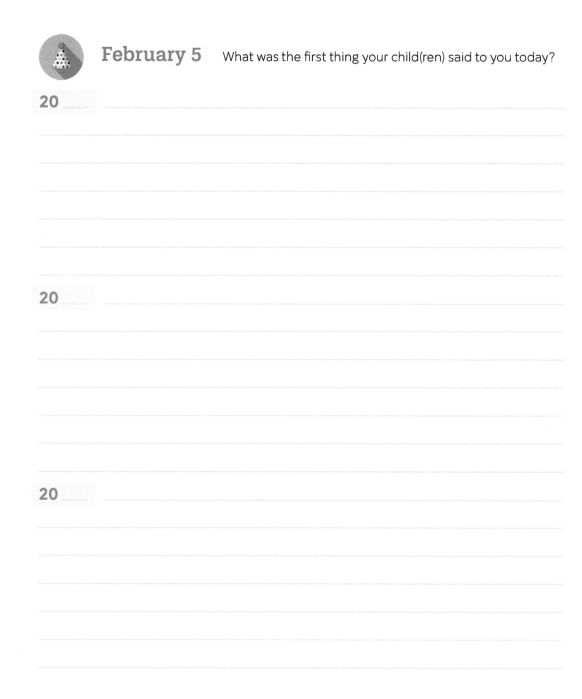

## February 5

What was the first thing your child(ren) said to you today?

**20**

**20**

**20**

## February 6

Last month, you wrote about how things changed for your family this past year. Now, consider this: How have things changed most for *you* this past year?

**20** _____

_____

_____

_____

_____

_____

**20** _____

_____

_____

_____

_____

_____

**20** _____

_____

_____

_____

_____

_____

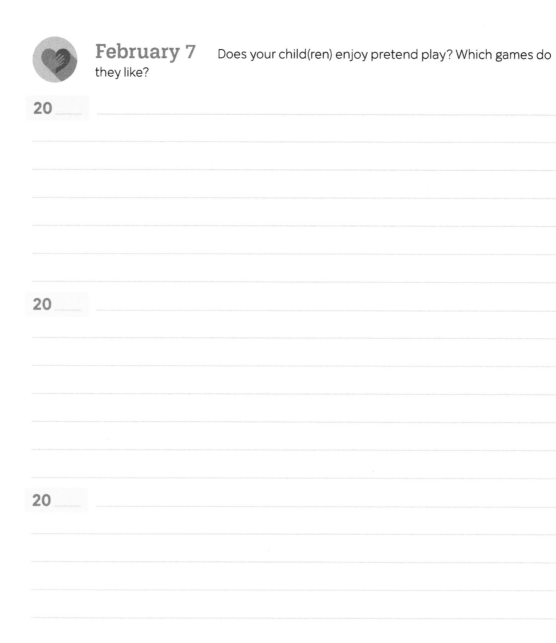

## February 7

Does your child(ren) enjoy pretend play? Which games do they like?

**20** ___

**20** ___

**20** ___

## February 8

Motherhood doesn't just change our day-to-day reality—it shapes us as people, too. How have you changed as a person since becoming a mom?

**20** _____

_____

_____

_____

_____

_____

**20** _____

_____

_____

_____

_____

_____

**20** _____

_____

_____

_____

_____

_____

## February 9
If you could set one goal for your family this year, what would it be?

20 _____ _____

_____

20 _____ _____

_____

20 _____ _____

_____


## February 10
What is the first kids' song that comes to your mind?

20 _____ _____

_____

20 _____ _____

_____

20 _____ _____

_____

## February 11
What new activity did you try as a family this past year? Would you do it again?

20 ___

20 ___

20 ___

## February 12
Does your child(ren) enjoy physical activity? Which exercises, games, or sports do they like?

20 ___

20 ___

20 ___

## February 13

What are some aspects of motherhood that were unexpected? What did each one teach you?

20 _____

20 _____

20 _____

## February 14

Where would you like to go on a family vacation in the coming year? Why?

20

20

20

## February 15
What silly thing does your child(ren) do to make you laugh? Do they do it on purpose or by accident?

**20**

_____

_____

**20**

_____

_____

**20**

_____

_____


## February 16
What were some of the books you enjoyed reading this past year? If you haven't had time to finish one, what's on your to-read list?

**20**

_____

_____

**20**

_____

_____

**20**

_____

_____

## February 17
Does your child(ren) enjoy trying new things, or do they prefer routine? Share a few examples.

20 _____

_____

_____

20 _____

_____

_____

20 _____

_____

_____


## February 18
What do you like most about being a mom?

20 _____

_____

_____

20 _____

_____

_____

20 _____

_____

_____

# February 19

When planning the coming year, what family events do you want to happen? Why would they be special to you?

**20**___ _____

**20**___ _____

**20**___ _____

## February 20

If you could build anything in the world for your child(ren), what would it be? Why did you pick that?

20 _____

20 _____

20 _____

## February 21
What were some of your child(ren)'s favorite books this past year?

20 _____

_____

20 _____

_____

20 _____

_____

## February 22
Is there something your child(ren) does not enjoy? It can be anything from riding in the car seat to eating spinach.

20 _____

_____

20 _____

_____

20 _____

_____

## February 23
What is something you have done as a mom that you never pictured yourself doing?

20 _____

20 _____

20 _____

## February 24
What mundane task are you looking forward to leaving behind as your child(ren) outgrows it?

20 _____

20 _____

20 _____

## February 25

If you could go anywhere in the world with your child(ren), where would you go and why? What would you want them to learn from the experience?

20____

20____

20____

## February 26 — What movies did you watch as a family in the past year?

20 _____

20 _____

20 _____

## February 27 — Is there something your child(ren) says that makes you laugh? It could be anything from the way they pronounce a certain word to a funny saying they have.

20 _____

20 _____

20 _____

## February 28

As rewarding as motherhood can be, it comes with many challenges. What are the things you find most difficult about being a mom? How can you work to overcome those challenges?

**20**

**20**

20

## March 1
What were your child(ren)'s favorite TV shows over this past year?

20 _____ _____

20 _____ _____

20 _____ _____

## March 2
What does your child(ren) enjoy wearing? It could be anything from certain colors to costumes or types of clothing.

20 _____ _____

20 _____ _____

20 _____ _____

## March 3
What is something you have said as a mom that you never imagined yourself saying?

20 _____

20 _____

20 _____

## March 4
What exciting new thing are you looking forward to your child(ren) being able to do this year?

20 _____

20 _____

20 _____

## March 5 — What is your favorite game to play with your child(ren)?

**20**

**20**

**20**

## March 6 — What were your favorite TV shows over this past year?

**20**

**20**

**20**

## March 7

What is a special way your child(ren) expresses themself? It could be anything from playing an instrument to dancing or drawing. What do you think it reveals about their character or personality?

**20**

**20**

**20**

## March 8
For International Women's Day today, what famous woman from history would you like to talk about with your child(ren)? What do you find interesting or admirable about her?

**20** _____

**20** _____

**20** _____

## March 9
Are there some family dates looming on the horizon this year that you are eager to check off the list? Maybe vaccinations or tests?

**20**

**20**

**20**

## March 10
If you could be any book character, who would you be?

**20**

**20**

**20**

## March 11

Did your child(ren) have a favorite teacher or childcare provider over this past year? What did they especially like about this person?

20 _____

20 _____

20 _____

## March 12

What always makes your child(ren) laugh?

20 _____

20 _____

20 _____

## March 13
Each season of motherhood brings new joys and challenges. How would you describe motherhood at this point in your journey?

20 _____ _____

_____

20 _____ _____

_____

20 _____ _____

_____


## March 14
What is a special skill or talent that you think your child(ren) will begin to learn or master this year? How do you see the acquisition of this new skill or talent affecting your child(ren) or family life?

20 _____ _____

_____

20 _____ _____

_____

20 _____ _____

_____

## March 15    What is your favorite thing about spring?

**20** ___

**20** ___

**20** ___

## March 16    What new activities did your child(ren) try this past year? Which did they like least and most?

**20** ___

**20** ___

**20** ___

**March 17**   What is your child(ren)'s special interest right now?

20 _____

20 _____

20 _____

**March 18**   What words of advice would you offer your pre-child self to help you prepare for motherhood?

20 _____

20 _____

20 _____

## March 19

What holiday are you most looking forward to celebrating with your child(ren) and why? How do you celebrate this holiday?

20 _____

_____

_____

_____

_____

_____

_____

20 _____

_____

_____

_____

_____

_____

_____

20 _____

_____

_____

_____

_____

_____

_____

# March 20

Describe the last time that your child(ren) made you laugh. What did they say or do?

**20**

**20**

**20**

**March 21** Did your child(ren) make any new friends over this past year? Share the name(s) of these friend(s) and where or how they met.

20 _____

20 _____

20 _____

**March 22** Does your child(ren) like to eat fruit? Which are their favorite and least favorite?

20 _____

20 _____

20 _____

## March 23
Have you noticed a change in your emotions since becoming a mother? What is different for you now?

20 _____

20 _____

20 _____

## March 24
Are there any exciting family dates on the horizon that you are looking forward to, such as summer camp or a trip?

20 _____

20 _____

20 _____

## March 25

If your kid(s) could make you dinner, what would you want them to cook for you?

**20**

**20**

**20**

## March 26

Have you and your child(ren) had the opportunity to visit with family members who don't live close by? Who did you visit? Where did the meeting take place, what did you do, and what made it special?

**20** _____

_____

_____

_____

_____

_____

**20** _____

_____

_____

_____

_____

_____

**20** _____

_____

_____

_____

_____

_____

## March 27
What does your child(ren) do that reminds you of yourself as a child?

**20** _____ _____

**20** _____ _____

**20** _____ _____

## March 28
Make sure you are getting some time to yourself to recharge! How do you enjoy spending your "me time"?

**20** _____ _____

**20** _____ _____

**20** _____ _____

## March 29
Looking ahead, what concerns do you have for the future? How will you handle or address these worries?

20 _____

20 _____

20 _____

## March 30
Think back to your last mommy blooper. What happened?

20 _____

20 _____

20 _____

## March 31

As your child(ren) grows, different traits and characteristics begin to emerge. What are the qualities you enjoy most about your child(ren)? (You may want to talk about different qualities each year.) Share a story or two about how you noticed them doing something that made you proud.

20

20

20

**April 1**   Children can be known for their strong food preferences and their sometimes fickle opinions. Is there a food that your child(ren) does not like? Are there foods they eat now but didn't like at first?

20 _____

_____

_____

20 _____

_____

_____

20 _____

_____

_____

_____

**April 2**   What is a challenging personality trait that you feel your child(ren) could work on overcoming? How do you think this would help them?

20 _____

_____

_____

20 _____

_____

_____

20 _____

_____

_____

**April 3**   What is a challenging personality trait that you could work on overcoming? How do you think this would help you?

**20** _____ _____

_____

**20** _____ _____

_____

**20** _____ _____

_____


**April 4**   What are some fun things you look forward to doing as a family when your child(ren) is a bit older?

**20** _____ _____

_____

**20** _____ _____

_____

**20** _____ _____

_____

## April 5

If you had to pick a family motto or catchphrase, what would it be and why?

20 _____

_____

_____

_____

_____

_____

20 _____

_____

_____

_____

_____

_____

20 _____

_____

_____

_____

_____

_____

## April 6

What new businesses opened near you during the past year or did you recently start supporting as a family? This is the perfect place to share anything from family favorite restaurants and what you all enjoy eating there to kids' play centers and what your kid(s) most enjoys doing there.

**20**

_____

_____

_____

_____

_____

**20**

_____

_____

_____

_____

_____

**20**

_____

_____

_____

_____

_____

**April 7**  What does your child(ren) want to be when they grow up? Do they change their mind frequently? Where do they seem to draw the inspiration for these career choices?

20

20

20

**April 8**  By what name (or sound) does your child(ren) call you?

20

20

20

## April 9
What do you all most look forward to doing as a family each weekend (or on your days off if you work a different schedule)?

20 _____ _____

_____

20 _____ _____

_____

20 _____ _____

_____


## April 10
What is your child(ren)'s favorite color?

20 _____ _____

_____

20 _____ _____

_____

20 _____ _____

_____

## April 11
Over this past year, what was a special experience that stands out for you?

**20** _____

_____

_____

**20** _____

_____

_____

**20** _____

_____

_____

## April 12
Kindness is such an important quality to foster. In what special ways does your child(ren) demonstrate kindness? How do you let them know you notice and appreciate their kind actions toward you or others?

**20** _____

_____

_____

**20** _____

_____

_____

**20** _____

_____

_____

### April 13
Becoming a mother often teaches us that we can't control every single thing. What expectations have you had to let go of? How has letting go of those expectations helped you grow as a person?

20

20

20

### April 14
Does your child(ren) have any childcare or school events coming up—for example, a book reading, magic show, holiday performance, or play? Be sure to note if they (or you) have a special role in the event.

20

20

20

**April 15**   If you could be any animal in the world, what would you be and why?

20 _____

20 _____

20 _____

**April 16**   Did you add any pets to the family during this past year? If so, write about them. If not, did your child(ren) show an interest in any particular animal(s) over the past year?

20 _____

20 _____

20 _____

## April 17
What is your child(ren)'s favorite hobby? If they are not old enough to have a real hobby yet, what do they most enjoy doing?

20____

20____

20____

## April 18
Sometimes it is helpful to have friends who are going through similar life changes at the same time as you. Have you made any new mom friends? What would you like to share with them?

20____

20____

20____

## April 19

What are some important lessons you would like to teach your kid(s) this year or important conversations you know you need to have? How do you plan to approach these subjects?

20\_\_\_\_

20\_\_\_\_

20\_\_\_\_

## April 20

Do you remember your first trip to the beach or a lake or pool, or your child(ren)'s first trip there? Share the memory that makes you the happiest.

**20** ___

_____

_____

_____

_____

_____

_____

**20** ___

_____

_____

_____

_____

_____

_____

_____

**20** ___

_____

_____

_____

_____

_____

_____

**April 21**   Did you visit a new place over this past year with your child(ren)? If you have several to choose from, write about the one with the best story around it.

20 _____

20 _____

20 _____

**April 22**   Does your child(ren) enjoy art? Do they like looking at it, creating it, or both? What medium is their favorite?

20 _____

20 _____

20 _____

## April 23
In what ways do you enjoy being creative? Examples may include home decor, crafts, cooking, needlework, or artwork. In what ways do you enjoy being creative with your child(ren)?

20 _____

20 _____

20 _____

## April 24
What career can you currently see your little one excelling at when they grow up? What are you basing this on—their current interests, personality traits, or the games they like to play?

20 _____

20 _____

20 _____

## April 25

If you won a million dollars, what would you do with the money and why?

20

20

20

**April 26**   Is there a person who has become an integral part of your family life during this past year? It could be anyone from a new neighborhood kid who is always at the dinner table to a live-in grandparent. Write a bit about this person and their role in your family life.

20 _____

_____

_____

_____

_____

_____

20 _____

_____

_____

_____

_____

_____

20 _____

_____

_____

_____

_____

_____

**April 27** Does your child(ren) enjoy trips to the library or bookstore? Write about what they do there and be sure to include any special classes or events for children that your local library offers. This is also a great place to record your child(ren)'s most recent favorite books.

20

20

20

## April 28 — What is one aspect of motherhood that you are grateful for?

20 _____

20 _____

20 _____

## April 29 — Is there a book you are eager to read to or with your child(ren) when they are older? It may be a favorite book from your childhood that you would like to introduce them to, or a special book you received as a gift.

20 _____

20 _____

20 _____

### April 30

Write about a perfect day with your kid(s). The part that makes this even more fun is you don't have any of the constraints of reality. So, for example, you could include teatime with the Queen of England or the Mad Hatter! Where would you go and what would you do?

20 ___

20 ___

**20**

**May 1**   What is one blessing you are thankful for from this past year and why?

20 _____

20 _____

20 _____

**May 2**   What is your child(ren)'s favorite meal? Do you think they would eat it every day if they could, or do they prefer variety?

20 _____

20 _____

20 _____

## May 3
What's your favorite mom job lately (for example, serving breakfast, bringing your kid(s) to the park, or tucking them in)? What do you enjoy about this job?

**20** _____

**20** _____

**20** _____

## May 4
How would you like to spend Mother's Day this year? Are you in the mood for adventure or rest? What would your perfect Mother's Day be like?

**20** _____

**20** _____

**20** _____

## May 5
What is something that is taught in school these days that is different from when you were a kid?

20 ____

20 ____

20 ____

## May 6
What are a few things your child(ren) seemed to enjoy about this school year that they may miss over the summer?

20 ____

20 ____

20 ____

## May 7

Which sports does your child(ren) like to play? Where do they get the opportunity to play them and what position do they play? If they don't like sports, what are some other physical activities that they enjoy, such as hiking?

20 _____

20 _____

20 _____

**May 8** Who supports you in your role as a mother, allowing you to be a better mom by lending a hand, ear, or a shoulder when you need it? Share a story or two of how their support lifts you up. (You may want to thank this person if you have been too busy to do so!)

20 _____

20 _____

20 _____

**May 9**  Schedules often look different over the summer. What changes in your family routine do you anticipate over the summer months?

20 _____ _____

_____

20 _____ _____

_____

20 _____ _____

_____


**May 10**  What is your feel-good song that you put on when you need a mood booster? What do you love about it?

20 _____ _____

_____

20 _____ _____

_____

20 _____ _____

_____

**May 11**    In what ways have you noticed your child(ren) becoming more independent over the past year?

20 _____ _____

_____

20 _____ _____

_____

20 _____ _____

_____


**May 12**    How much time does your child(ren) spend on homework each day, on average? Do they do their homework on their own, or do they need reminding?

20 _____ _____

_____

20 _____ _____

_____

20 _____ _____

_____

**May 13**  What do you think is the perfect number of children for you as a mother and why?

20____

_____

_____

_____

_____

_____

_____

20____

_____

_____

_____

_____

_____

_____

_____

20____

_____

_____

_____

_____

_____

_____

## May 14

What are some changes that you anticipate making to your house or to your child(ren)'s room as they grow?

**20** _____

_____

_____

_____

_____

_____

**20** _____

_____

_____

_____

_____

_____

**20** _____

_____

_____

_____

_____

_____

**May 15**   What is your favorite thing about this time of year?

20

20

20

**May 16**   Write about any memorable weather events over this past year. Did they affect your family, and if so, how?

20

20

20

## May 17
Record your child(ren)'s progress in learning how to ride a bike. If they haven't started on a bike yet, what is their favorite ride-on toy right now? If this is a skill they have already mastered, what are their bike adventures like? Do they ride around the neighborhood, to school, or on bike trails?

20 _____

20 _____

20 _____

## May 18
What is one aspect of motherhood that came easily to you? Why do you think that is?

20 _____

20 _____

20 _____

## May 19

Family meetings can be useful for keeping everyone organized and on the same page with important information and goals. What would you like to discuss in your next family meeting? Share several things—from talking about family values, to planning after-school routines, to discussing chores.

**20**

**20**

**20**

### May 20

Being a mom is a wonderful experience, but it can be easy to get lost in it. Looking back over this past year, do you feel you are balancing being a mom with other areas that are important to you? What are you doing well and where do you want to apply a little more attention or effort?

**20** _____

_____

_____

_____

_____

_____

**20** _____

_____

_____

_____

_____

_____

**20** _____

_____

_____

_____

_____

_____

**May 21** What kind of after-school routine did you have this year? Did it work well for you? Are there any ways you would like to tweak it for next year?

20 ___

___

20 ___

___

20 ___

___

**May 22** Does your child(ren) help with chores? How do they pitch in to help the whole household run more smoothly?

20 ___

___

20 ___

___

20 ___

___

**May 23**   If you could delegate one of your roles as mom to someone else, which one would it be and why?

20 ___

20 ___

20 ___

**May 24**   Is there something you dream of doing as soon as you get a moment to yourself? What is it?

20 ___

20 ___

20 ___

## May 25

What is your favorite way to relax and unwind? Describe what an evening of fun without your kid(s) would look like for you.

**20** _____

**20** _____

**20** _____

### May 26

Did you explore any new places for outdoor fun during this past year? Where did you go and what did you do there?

20____

_____

_____

_____

_____

_____

20____

_____

_____

_____

_____

_____

20____

_____

_____

_____

_____

_____

## May 27
Bossy? The voice of reason? A mediator? What role does each child currently play in your family? Provide a few examples.

20___

20___

20___

## May 28
How would you characterize the way that you mother? Do you run a dictatorship or a democracy? Are there exceptions to the rule?

20___

20___

20___

**May 29**  What are some changes you would like to make to your family schedule to have more quality time together? This may involve cutting out a few activities to create more downtime, or it may include your child(ren) helping with chores so that you have more free time to spend with them.

**20**

**20**

**20**

**May 30**  What is the most surprising thing your child(ren) has done so far?

**20**

**20**

**20**

## May 31

Sometimes looking ahead can help us take advantage of our time right now. Try looking into the future and anticipating any major changes you see coming your way in the next year. What do you find yourself wishing for? List three things that come to mind and what you will do to prepare for them. For example, maybe you feel like time is flying by and you want to take more photos and capture these special moments now.

20

20

20

### June 1 — What is an experience from this past year that you really enjoyed?

**20** _____

_____

**20** _____

_____

**20** _____

_____


### June 2 — What is a cute pronunciation of a word or their very own saying that your child(ren) uses?

**20** _____

_____

**20** _____

_____

**20** _____

_____

**June 3**   What worries you most about being a mom?

20 _____

20 _____

20 _____

**June 4**   What is one lesson that you have learned? How would you use it to make better choices in the future?

20 _____

20 _____

20 _____

## June 5

What is something you would invent to make motherhood easier?

**20**

**20**

**20**

### June 6

Every year is full of ups and downs. What was a rough spot during this past year? What did you learn from it or how did it make you grow as a person?

**20** ___

**20** ___

**20** ___

**June 7** Children need to be taught about emotions and how to communicate feelings. Does your child(ren) seem to know what they are feeling and why? What emotion is challenging them right now? How might you help them work through those feelings?

20 _____

20 _____

20 _____

**June 8**    At this stage, what is the scariest part of being a mom?

20 ____

20 ____

20 ____

**June 9**    Do you have a passion or a hobby that you look forward to sharing with your child(ren)? How would you like to introduce them to it or give them a deeper appreciation for what it is all about?

20 ____

20 ____

20 ____

**June 10**   What music do you enjoy listening to right now?

20 _____

20 _____

20 _____

**June 11**   What is one lesson that you are grateful for so far this year?

20 _____

20 _____

20 _____

## June 12

Record your child(ren)'s reading progress. Share all the details! Does your child(ren) enjoy reading?

**20** ___

**20** ___

**20** ___

## June 13

How has being a mother made you a better person?

**20** _____

_____

_____

_____

_____

_____

**20** _____

_____

_____

_____

_____

_____

**20** _____

_____

_____

_____

_____

_____

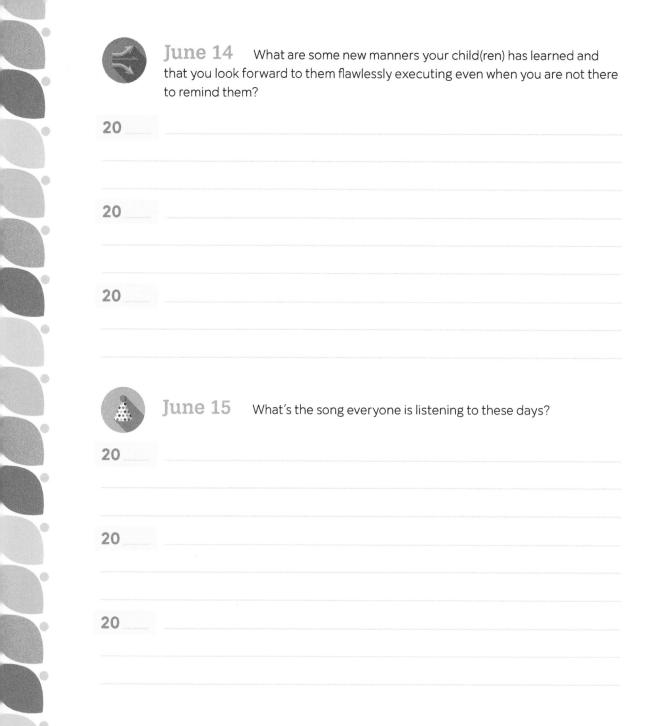

## June 14

What are some new manners your child(ren) has learned and that you look forward to them flawlessly executing even when you are not there to remind them?

20 _____

20 _____

20 _____

## June 15

What's the song everyone is listening to these days?

20 _____

20 _____

20 _____

**June 16**  How will everything that has happened this past year build an even stronger foundation for your family?

20 _____ _____

_____

20 _____ _____

_____

20 _____ _____

_____


**June 17**  What is your child(ren)'s favorite school subject and why? If they aren't in school yet, what do they seem most curious about?

20 _____ _____

_____

20 _____ _____

_____

20 _____ _____

_____

## June 18

What is a recent mothering moment that you would like to record for you and your child(ren) to remember later? It can be anything from a day volunteering in the classroom and what your child(ren) said about it to a conversation you had with your child(ren) where you were able to guide their thoughts around something important.

20___

20___

20___

## June 19
Most children tend to have more free time over the summer. How would you like your child(ren) to spend their extra free time? How will you guide their choices?

**20**

**20**

**20**

## June 20

What are three ways you have fun?

**20** _____

_____

**20** _____

_____

**20** _____

_____

## June 21

What areas of life were you most focused on this past year?

**20** _____

_____

**20** _____

_____

**20** _____

_____

## June 22

What is something thoughtful that your child(ren) has done for you lately?

20 _____ _____

_____

20 _____ _____

_____

20 _____ _____

_____

## June 23

What are some of the perks of being a mom?

20 _____ _____

_____

20 _____ _____

_____

20 _____ _____

_____

## June 24

What is the next family outing you would like to plan? Who will go along and what will you do?

**20** ___

**20** ___

**20** ___

## June 25

Are you more of an introvert or an extrovert? How do you know?

**20** ___

**20** ___

**20** ___

## June 26
In this past year, have you been camping or hiking? If so, write about it here. If not, would you like to go? Where?

20____

20____

20____

## June 27
What similarities do you see between your children, or between your child and another family member?

20____

20____

20____

## June 28
When you are feeling low, what do you do to motivate yourself and feel better?

**20**

**20**

**20**

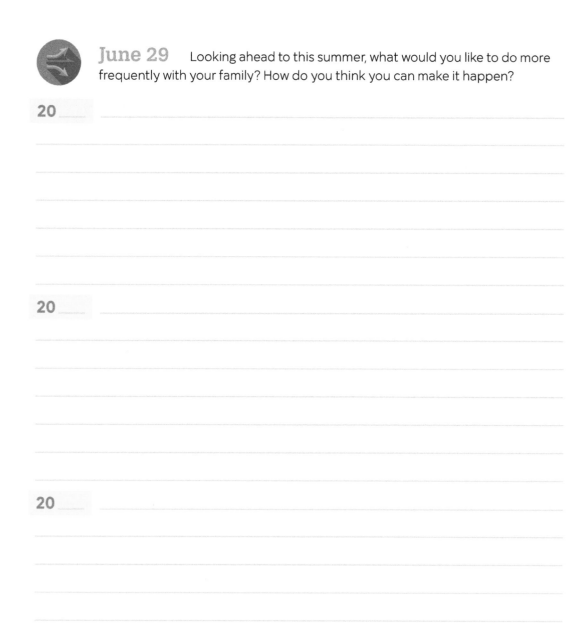

June 29    Looking ahead to this summer, what would you like to do more frequently with your family? How do you think you can make it happen?

**20** ___

**20** ___

**20** ___

## June 30

When thinking about this past year, what would you most like to change? Why do you want to change this, and how can you work toward doing so?

**20** ____

_____

_____

_____

_____

_____

_____

_____

_____

_____

_____

_____

_____

**20** ____

_____

_____

_____

_____

_____

20

**July 1**   What new guilty pleasure did you discover over this past year? When do you take the time to indulge in it?

20 _____ _____

_____

20 _____ _____

_____

20 _____ _____

_____


**July 2**   Does your child(ren) have a pet peeve? What is it lately?

20 _____ _____

_____

20 _____ _____

_____

20 _____ _____

_____

**July 3**    Do you have a pet peeve? What is it lately?

20 ___

20 ___

20 ___

**July 4**    What do you want to do less of this month?

20 ___

20 ___

20 ___

## July 5   What movie made you laugh or moved you to tears recently?

**20** ___

**20** ___

**20** ___

## July 6   Looking back at this past year, what area of life would you most like to work on improving? What small step can you take to start on that path?

**20** ___

**20** ___

**20** ___

## July 7

Describe your child(ren)'s sleep habits. Are they excellent sleepers, or do they wake up several times a night? Do they hop into your bed, or have they outgrown that? Do they have any special good-night routines?

**20** _____

**20** _____

**20** _____

## July 8

Motherhood is a demanding job even at its best. It's important to give yourself plenty of credit and cheer yourself on. What about motherhood makes you most proud?

**20** _____

_____

_____

_____

_____

**20** _____

_____

_____

_____

_____

**20** _____

_____

_____

_____

_____

**July 9**   Are you and your family enjoying any summer activities that you want to squeeze in more of before school starts?

20

20

20

**July 10**   How do you recharge?

20

20

20

## July 11 Who is a new music artist you like this year?

**20** _____ _____

_____

**20** _____ _____

_____

**20** _____ _____

_____

## July 12 Who is your child(ren)'s best friend this year? What do they enjoy doing together?

**20** _____ _____

_____

**20** _____ _____

_____

**20** _____ _____

_____

## July 13
Write about a time when you felt particularly good at being a mother and you knew you were doing something right! What happened and what made you feel good?

20

20

20

## July 14
Given the character and personality of your child(ren) at this time, what hobbies or interests do you imagine they will have as an adult(s)?

20

20

20

## July 15 What is your favorite thing about summer?

**20** _____

**20** _____

**20** _____

## July 16 What new talent did you discover in yourself this past year?

**20** _____

**20** _____

**20** _____

**July 17**   Each of us has different motivational drives. What motivates your child(ren) at this stage of their life?

20 _____

_____

_____

20 _____

_____

_____

20 _____

_____

_____


**July 18**   Parenting sometimes feels like it comes naturally and that the right thing to do or say is obvious. Other times, it can leave you second-guessing yourself. Where do you go for advice? Who do you talk to for parenting tips?

20 _____

_____

_____

20 _____

_____

_____

20 _____

_____

_____

## July 19

What's something precious you learned from your grandparents or anyone in that generation? How do you plan to teach this to your child(ren)?

**20** ___

_____

_____

_____

_____

_____

_____

**20** ___

_____

_____

_____

_____

_____

_____

**20** ___

_____

_____

_____

_____

_____

_____

## July 20

What do you like to do on a rainy day? List your top five choices and add details.

**20**

**20**

**20**

## July 21

What is the best piece of advice you received over this past year?

20 _____

_____

20 _____

_____

20 _____

_____

## July 22

What size shoe does your child(ren) wear right now?

20 _____

_____

20 _____

_____

20 _____

_____

### July 23

How do you show your family you love them?

**20** ____

**20** ____

**20** ____

### July 24

What is your family's favorite way to enjoy water? Is it a trip to the beach, a nearby lake, or a pool? Or is it just a run through the sprinklers?

**20** ____

**20** ____

**20** ____

## July 25
What's something that your child(ren) would be surprised to learn about you? Why do you think this would surprise them?

**20**

**20**

**20**

## July 26

It is so great to have someone to talk to about the things that are important to you. Who has been your closest confidant over this past year? What qualities make them such a good friend?

**20**

**20**

**20**

**July 27**  Does your child(ren) have any nicknames? What terms of endearment do different people use for them?

20

20

20

**July 28**  In what ways do you see yourself in your child(ren)?

20

20

20

**July 29**  Are there any favorite summer dishes you would like to squeeze in a few more times? Which family members are partial to which dishes?

20 ___

20 ___

20 ___

**July 30**  What is a funny story your child(ren) told you recently? Did it actually happen, or did they make it up?

20 ___

20 ___

20 ___

**July 31**  As a mother, what two values do you most want to teach your child(ren) at this stage? Why do you consider these values to be so important? In what ways will you try to teach them to your child(ren)? Do you have a life experience story you will share with them to illustrate how these values serve you well in life or how ignoring them can work out poorly?

**20** _____

_____

_____

_____

_____

_____

_____

_____

_____

_____

_____

_____

**20** _____

_____

_____

_____

_____

20

**August 1**   What is the most fun you've had over the summer so far?

20 _____

20 _____

20 _____

**August 2**   Do you think your child(ren) will enjoy starting school either for the first time or again this year? What part of it do you think they will enjoy—or not?

20 _____

20 _____

20 _____

## August 3
Motherhood is constantly changing as your child(ren) grows and develops. What areas of motherhood seem to be in flux at the moment?

**20** _____

**20** _____

**20** _____

## August 4
What would you like to do on your next free weekend? Who would you like to spend time with?

**20** _____

**20** _____

**20** _____

## August 5
Share a random story from your own childhood. What comes to mind first?

**20** _____

_____

_____

**20** _____

_____

_____

**20** _____

_____

_____

## August 6
What activity did you find most beneficial for building a strong family bond over the past year?

**20** _____

_____

_____

**20** _____

_____

_____

**20** _____

_____

_____

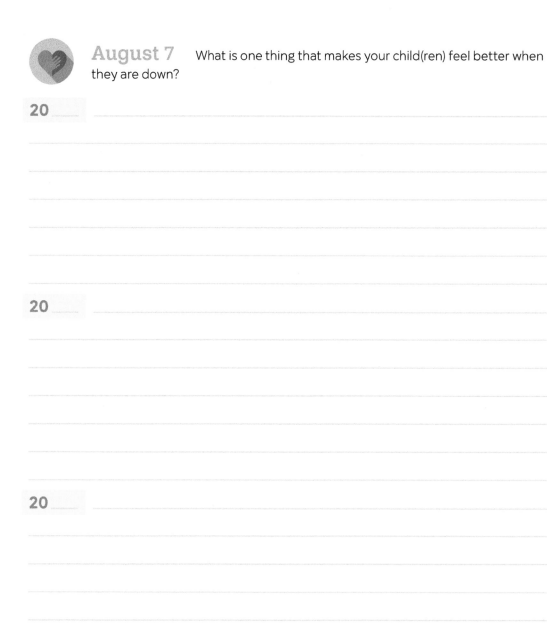

## August 7

What is one thing that makes your child(ren) feel better when they are down?

**20** _____

_____

_____

_____

_____

_____

**20** _____

_____

_____

_____

_____

_____

**20** _____

_____

_____

_____

_____

_____

## August 8

In what ways has your appreciation for motherhood grown now that you are a mother yourself?

20_____

20_____

20_____

## August 9

What are some things you would like to accomplish as a mother?

20 _____

20 _____

20 _____

## August 10

Who is your hero and why?

20 _____

20 _____

20 _____

## August 11
In what ways have you taught your child(ren) about their unique heritage during the past year?

20 _____

_____

20 _____

_____

20 _____

_____

## August 12
Who is your child(ren)'s hero and what do they like about this person or character?

20 _____

_____

20 _____

_____

20 _____

_____

## August 13

In what ways has being a mother stretched and grown your talents?

20____

20____

20____

## August 14

With school coming up, what do you need to do to prepare? Make a list!

**20** _____

**20** _____

**20** _____

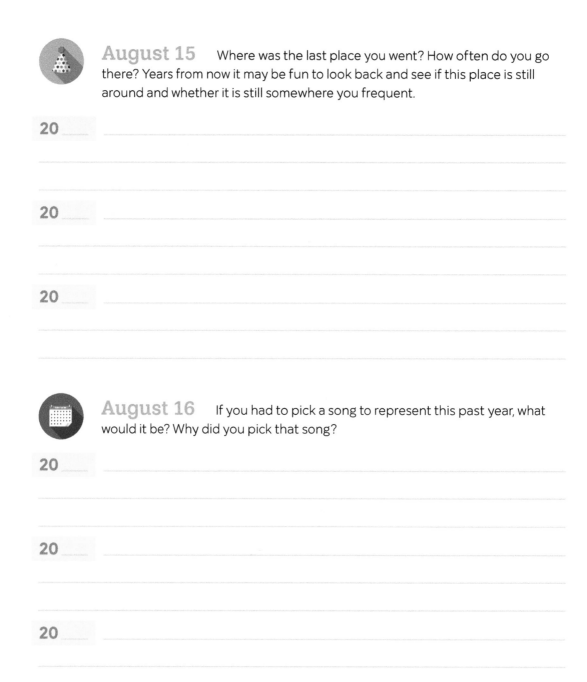

### August 15
Where was the last place you went? How often do you go there? Years from now it may be fun to look back and see if this place is still around and whether it is still somewhere you frequent.

20 _____

20 _____

20 _____

### August 16
If you had to pick a song to represent this past year, what would it be? Why did you pick that song?

20 _____

20 _____

20 _____

## August 17    What is your child(ren)'s favorite song to listen to right now?

**20** _____

**20** _____

**20** _____

## August 18    Have you developed any new hobbies since becoming a mother? Write about your new hobby or a hobby you'd like to try.

**20** _____

**20** _____

**20** _____

**August 19**   Sometimes being a mom can feel overwhelming, and it may be a good idea to ask for or hire some help. What are some areas you could use help with?

**20** _____

**20** _____

**20** _____

## August 20

If you could have a vacation home anywhere, where would it be and why?

**20** _____

**20** _____

**20** _____

**August 21**  What is one lesson you think your child(ren) learned during this past year?

20 ____

20 ____

20 ____

**August 22**  What is one thing you love about your child(ren)? Each year, pick something different and write about a recent memory in which they demonstrated this quality.

20 ____

20 ____

20 ____

## August 23
What is something you are particularly enjoying about motherhood right now?

20 _____

_____

_____

20 _____

_____

_____

20 _____

_____

_____


## August 24
In what ways will your schedule change as your child(ren) goes back to school?

20 _____

_____

_____

20 _____

_____

_____

20 _____

_____

_____

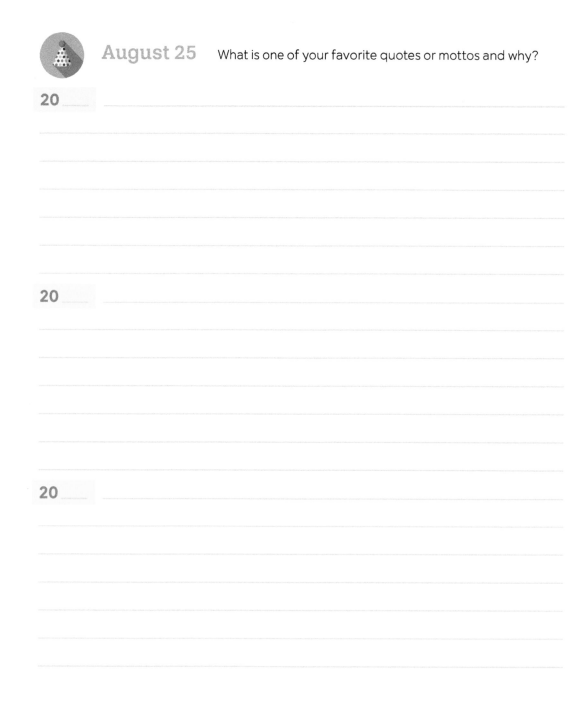

## August 25

What is one of your favorite quotes or mottos and why?

**20**

**20**

**20**

## August 26

When you look back at this past year, what makes you feel inspired? What does this inspire you to achieve or do?

**20**

**20**

**20**

## August 27
Is your child(ren) planning to try any new extracurricular activities this year? Are there any that you are encouraging them to try? What traits do you see in your kid(s) that might make them a particularly good match for a certain club or activity?

**20**

**20**

**20**

## August 28
What is something that you find challenging about motherhood right now? Don't forget, it's okay to seek help when you need it!

**20**

**20**

**20**

**August 29**   What is something you are eager to teach your child(ren) so they can pitch in around the house more?

20 _____

_____

_____

20 _____

_____

_____

20 _____

_____

_____

_____

**August 30**   Would you like to visit the moon if you could? Why or why not?

20 _____

_____

_____

20 _____

_____

_____

20 _____

_____

_____

## August 31

What is a new skill that you have enjoyed watching your child(ren) work to learn or improve? Share what you enjoy about them learning this new skill. How do you think mastering this will be beneficial for them or others?

**20**

**20**

20

## September 1
What is something your child(ren) has struggled with over the past year? How have you and your child(ren) worked to persevere and overcome this?

20 _____

20 _____

20 _____

## September 2
What gifts does your child(ren) enjoy most? Have they had a favorite this past year?

20 _____

20 _____

20 _____

## September 3
Is there a trait that you wish you had more of as a mother? How would that make motherhood easier or more fun?

20 _____

20 _____

20 _____

## September 4
What is one area of improvement that you would like to work on this month? It can be in any category—in your home, in your kid(s), in yourself, in your career, or anything else.

20 _____

20 _____

20 _____

## September 5

What superpowers would you like to have? How would you use these powers to have fun or make the world a better place?

**20**

**20**

**20**

## September 6

In what ways has this been a good year for your family?

**20**

**20**

**20**

## September 7

In what ways has your child(ren) changed over the past year?

20_____

20_____

20_____

## September 8
Is there something about motherhood that caught you off guard? In what ways have you had to adjust your expectations?

20 _____

20 _____

20 _____

## September 9
What is an autumn activity that you are eager to enjoy with your family?

20 _____

20 _____

20 _____

## September 10

Do you have any nicknames? Who calls you by what name?

20

20

20

## September 11

What is a favorite craft that your child(ren) made over this past year?

20

20

20

## September 12

Would you describe your child(ren) as outgoing, shy, or somewhere in the middle? What advice have you given to help them work on their social skills?

**20**

**20**

**20**

## September 13

Are you an introvert or an extrovert? How do you think this plays a role in the way you mother?

**20** ___

**20** ___

**20** ___

## September 14

What fall food are you looking forward to having with your family?

20 ___

20 ___

20 ___

## September 15

What is one of the best gifts you have received this year? What did you like about it?

20 ___

20 ___

20 ___

## September 16
What is the best thing you can remember eating this past year? Where did you have it and what did you love about it?

**20** _____

_____

_____

**20** _____

_____

_____

**20** _____

_____

_____

## September 17
What does your child(ren) enjoy giving you? It could be something as simple as a hug, a bouquet, or a card. Write about a memory of this from the past year.

**20** _____

_____

_____

**20** _____

_____

_____

**20** _____

_____

_____

## September 18

What are you grateful for about motherhood and why?

**20**

**20**

**20**

## September 19

What do you look forward to doing with your kid(s) later in life when they are an adult(s)?

20____

20____

20____

## September 20 — What is your child(ren)'s favorite animal and why?

**20** _____

_____

**20** _____

_____

**20** _____

_____

## September 21 — What was one of the most fun family activities you have done together over the past year?

**20** _____

_____

**20** _____

_____

**20** _____

_____

## September 22
What is your child(ren)'s favorite cartoon right now? What do they like about it?

20

20

20

## September 23
What do you do to make your child(ren) feel better when they are sad?

20

20

20

## September 24

We all get overscheduled sometimes. Is there anything you could eliminate from your schedule in the next month that would free up more family time? What would you like to do with that time together?

20

20

20

## September 25

What shiny new gadget has captured your attention lately? What would you use it for and how would it make your life better or easier?

**20**

**20**

**20**

## September 26 — What fall activities have you done as a family so far?

**20** _____ _____

_____

**20** _____ _____

_____

**20** _____ _____

_____

## September 27 — Does your child(ren) like to help in the kitchen or watch you cook? What are their favorite things to make or taste as you make them?

**20** _____ _____

_____

**20** _____ _____

_____

**20** _____ _____

_____

## September 28
What activities do you give your kid(s) to do when you need a little bit of you time?

20 _____

20 _____

20 _____

## September 29
What does your family do to welcome the fall?
Do you have a tradition of special fall plantings, door wreaths, or seasonal table settings? Does your child(ren) help by making seasonal crafts to display?

20 _____

20 _____

20 _____

## September 30

Just for fun, imagine your child(ren)'s future! Write about where they will live, what career they will have, and what their family will look like. It will be fun to see how this compares to real life down the road.

**20**

**20**

20

## October 1

What were a few unexpected blessings your family received over this past year?

**20**___

**20**___

**20**___

## October 2

What is your child(ren) struggling with right now? What tools do you think you can help them with so they can get past this?

**20** ___

**20** ___

**20** ___

## October 3
What kind of mother did you think you would be? What kind of mother have you found yourself to be?

20 _____

_____

_____

20 _____

_____

_____

20 _____

_____

_____


## October 4
What is something you hope to accomplish this month?

20 _____

_____

_____

20 _____

_____

_____

20 _____

_____

_____

## October 5 — What is your favorite new recipe that you have made lately?

**20** ___

**20** ___

**20** ___

## October 6 — What are some family activities you enjoyed in the warm weather that you have begun to cut out now as it grows colder? How will you replace these?

**20** ___

**20** ___

**20** ___

## October 7
If you were to describe your child(ren) to an old friend you haven't seen in a while, what would you say about them?

20 _____

20 _____

20 _____

## October 8
What qualities do you show when you're mothering that you find hard to show when you're not? Write about a few examples.

**20**

**20**

**20**

**October 9**  What is a positive trait of yours that you would like to pass on to your child(ren)? Why is this important to you?

20___

_____

_____

20___

_____

_____

20___

_____

_____


**October 10**  What inspires you? It could be a person, a subject of interest, or anything at all that makes you feel passionate and excited about possibilities.

20___

_____

_____

20___

_____

_____

20___

_____

_____

**October 11**  Have you been to any fall festivals yet, or are you planning to attend any? Share some of the highlights you enjoyed or that you are looking forward to.

20 _____

20 _____

20 _____

**October 12**  How often does your child(ren) outgrow their clothing?

20 _____

20 _____

20 _____

## October 13

Our ideas and expectations for the future are often changing. Before you had your child(ren), how many children did you think you would want and why? How many do you think you want now and why?

20____

_____

_____

_____

_____

_____

_____

20____

_____

_____

_____

_____

_____

_____

20____

_____

_____

_____

_____

_____

_____

## October 14

What winter activities do you look forward to doing with your family? Do they require travel? Have you all done them before, or will these be first-time experiences?

**20** _____

**20** _____

**20** _____

## October 15
What is the last movie you watched, and what did you like or dislike about it?

20

20

20

## October 16
What is something special you did this past year that you would like to do again?

20

20

20

## October 17
Does your child(ren) bicker with their sibling(s) or friends? What do they usually argue about?

**20** ____

**20** ____

**20** ____

## October 18
What's your mommy motto or a quote about motherhood that you enjoy? If you don't have one, try to think one up or choose one now.

**20** ____

**20** ____

**20** ____

## October 19

What are your plans for this weekend?

**20**

**20**

**20**

**October 20** If you were to make an ice cream sundae for each member of your family, what do you think each person would want?

20____

20____

20____

**October 21** Practice makes perfect. What is something a family member has been practicing over the past year and has shown great improvement in?

20

20

20

**October 22** We all make mistakes, and it's important that we learn from them. What is a mistake that your child(ren) made recently that they were able to learn from?

20

20

20

## October 23

Who do you connect with most as a mother? Who listens to your mom stories and relates?

20 _____

20 _____

20 _____

## October 24

There are only a few months left in the year. What are some activities you would like to squeeze in before the year is done?

20 _____

20 _____

20 _____

## October 25

Describe a person who was important to your childhood. How did they influence you?

**20**

**20**

**20**

## October 26

In what ways have you enjoyed watching your child(ren) grow over this past year? What do you think encouraged this growth?

20 ___

20 ___

20 ___

## October 27
What is on your child(ren)'s mind this week? What are some recent stories they shared or questions they asked?

**20** ____

**20** ____

**20** ____

## October 28
What is on your mind this week?

**20** ____

**20** ____

**20** ____

## October 29
What is your child(ren)'s favorite costume to dress up in this year?

**20** ____

**20** ____

**20** ____

## October 30
If you could go anywhere and do anything right now, what would it be and who would you do it with?

**20** ____

**20** ____

**20** ____

## October 31

Think about your future hopes and dreams for your child(ren). How can you help prepare them?

**20**

_____

**20**

_____

20

# November 1
What is a meal that stands out in your memory from this past year because your child(ren) helped make it? Write about it here.

**20** _____

_____

**20** _____

_____

**20** _____

_____

# November 2
What makes your child(ren) happy?

**20** _____

_____

**20** _____

_____

**20** _____

_____

## November 3    What makes you happy?

**20** _____

_____

_____

**20** _____

_____

_____

**20** _____

_____

_____

## November 4    What concerns you about your child(ren)'s future? Do you plan to share those concerns with them?

**20** _____

_____

_____

**20** _____

_____

_____

**20** _____

_____

_____

## November 5

Have you done any family history research? Write what you know about your family tree here. Try to add some new information each year.

**20**

**20**

**20**

## November 6

Is there a special memory that may have gone unrecorded during this past year? Share all the details now.

20____

20____

20____

## November 7

Here is your chance to brag about your child(ren)'s latest accomplishments. What are you proud of them about? It can be anything from a pretty finger painting to an academic award.

20 _____

_____

_____

_____

_____

_____

20 _____

_____

_____

_____

_____

_____

20 _____

_____

_____

_____

_____

_____

### November 8
If you were to brag about yourself as a mother (and we all deserve a pat on the back sometimes), what would you say?

**20** _____

**20** _____

**20** _____

### November 9
How will you celebrate Thanksgiving? Will you enlist helpers for a feast at home? Will you be traveling?

**20** _____

**20** _____

**20** _____

## November 10
If you were to open a gift box right now, what one thing would you want to find inside?

**20** _____

_____

**20** _____

_____

**20** _____

_____

## November 11
How does your child(ren) help you out? Do they have any chores or responsibilities? What thoughtful things do they do?

**20** _____

_____

**20** _____

_____

**20** _____

_____

## November 12

What qualities do you see in your child(ren) that you are most thankful for?

20_____

20_____

20_____

## November 13

Moms tend to have a lot of responsibilities within the family. What are your various roles?

**20**

**20**

**20**

## November 14
What special foods will you prepare for the Thanksgiving feast? How do they connect with your heritage? Does each family member have a favorite dish?

**20** ___

**20** ___

**20** ___

## November 15
What toppings did you get on the last pizza you ate? Does your child(ren) have a favorite topping?

**20** ___

**20** ___

**20** ___

## November 16
Do you make scrapbooks or photo albums? How did you record your family memories over this past year?

20 _____

20 _____

20 _____

## November 17
Thinking of your child(ren)'s best friend right now, what qualities do you believe your child(ren) enjoys about this person?

20 _____

20 _____

20 _____

## November 18

In what ways is motherhood the best thing that ever happened to you?

20____

20____

20____

## November 19

In what ways do you think your family will grow and change over the next year?

20

20

20

## November 20
Answer a different question each year: What is your spirit animal? Who is your kindred spirit? Who is your celebrity twin?

20 ___

20 ___

20 ___

## November 21
Reflecting on this past year, what would you have done differently?

20 ___

20 ___

20 ___

## November 22
When do you think your child(ren) feels most loved? What makes them glow with satisfaction?

20 _____

_____

20 _____

_____

20 _____

_____

## November 23
When do you feel most loved? What does your child(ren) do or say that makes your heart feel full?

20 _____

_____

20 _____

_____

20 _____

_____

## November 24

What winter crafts do you look forward to? Where do you get your crafting ideas, and how do you display the finished products?

20 _____

_____

_____

_____

_____

_____

20 _____

_____

_____

_____

_____

_____

20 _____

_____

_____

_____

_____

_____

## November 25

If you were super handy, what would you build for yourself to make things easier? How would this addition be helpful?

20

20

20

## November 26
What is something you or your child(ren) worked hard to overcome this past year? Make sure to give yourself or your child(ren) the praise they deserve for this accomplishment.

20 _____

_____

_____

20 _____

_____

_____

20 _____

_____

_____

## November 27
Ask your child(ren) to share a story from their day. What did they tell you?

20 _____

_____

_____

20 _____

_____

_____

20 _____

_____

_____

## November 28
Share a random mothering story from your day. What happened? This is meant for you to record little moments of what mothering is like, so it doesn't have to be a special story or a huge memorable event.

20 _____

20 _____

20 _____

## November 29
Only one month left in the year! What do you need to put on your to-do list before the year ends?

20 _____

20 _____

20 _____

## November 30

What are the very best parts of being a mother at this particular stage? Write down all the things you love so you don't forget any details!

**20** _____

**20** _____

20

### December 1

During this past year, did anything happen that scared your kid(s)? How did you comfort them?

**20** _____

**20** _____

**20** _____

# December 2

What is something creative that your child(ren) made recently (such as art, a craft, a science project, or food)? Where did they get the idea? How did they share it with you?

20 _____

_____

_____

_____

_____

_____

_____

20 _____

_____

_____

_____

_____

_____

_____

20 _____

_____

_____

_____

_____

_____

_____

## December 3
What is something you are using your mothering skills to help your child(ren) improve in?

20____

20____

20____

## December 4
December tends to be an incredibly busy month. Looking ahead, are there any optional obligations that you could clear out of your schedule to make sure you are getting quality family time? Or is there a way to involve your kid(s) with something on your to-do list to make it fun for everyone?

20____

20____

20____

## December 5 — What did you do for fun today?

20 _____

20 _____

20 _____

## December 6 — What was your child(ren)'s favorite birthday present this past year?

20 _____

20 _____

20 _____

## December 7

What is your child(ren)'s favorite song to sing right now? Where did they learn the song? Why do they like it?

**20**____ _____

_____

_____

_____

_____

**20**____ _____

_____

_____

_____

_____

**20**____ _____

_____

_____

_____

_____

## December 8

At this stage of motherhood, how do you feel about sleepovers? If your child(ren) has sleepovers, do they have any special routines or foods that are part of the fun?

20 ___

_____

_____

_____

_____

_____

_____

_____

20 ___

_____

_____

_____

_____

_____

_____

_____

20 ___

_____

_____

_____

_____

_____

_____

_____

## December 9
What holidays or traditions do you celebrate this time of the year? Write about any upcoming big events for your family.

20 _____ _____

_____

20 _____ _____

_____

20 _____ _____

_____


## December 10
If you could try out a new career right now, what would you want to do?

20 _____ _____

_____

20 _____ _____

_____

20 _____ _____

_____

### December 11

Did your child(ren) build any cool forts, tents, or play-houses this year? What materials did they use, and what games do they like to play in their "building"?

**20**

**20**

**20**

### December 12

If your child(ren) had to pick one thing they love most in their room, what would it be and why?

**20**

**20**

**20**

## December 13

What is the funniest part of being a mom? Share some examples.

**20**___

**20**___

**20**___

## December 14

What special foods do you or your family make at this time of the year? Who do you make them for? Where did you learn about these dishes?

**20**

**20**

**20**

## December 15    What is the last photo you took? Describe it.

**20**

**20**

**20**

## December 16    Sometimes getting the whole family together in one photo is hard. Did you manage to get some family photos this past year? If not, write about how you will make that happen.

**20**

**20**

**20**

## December 17
What is your child(ren)'s favorite thing to do on your or their cell phone?

20 _____

_____

20 _____

_____

20 _____

_____

## December 18
It's important to find self-care practices that work for you. How do you practice self-care when you are feeling exhausted?

20 _____

_____

20 _____

_____

20 _____

_____

## December 19

What would you like to add to your current routine? What would you like to remove?

20____

20____

20____

## December 20

What's something funny that recently made you laugh out loud?

**20** ____

**20** ____

**20** ____

## December 21
How do you measure the success of this past year? Be sure to spot the silver linings!

20

20

20

## December 22
Does your child(ren) like to eat vegetables? Which ones are their favorite and least favorite?

20

20

20

## December 23
As a mother, do you see some of your own parents in yourself? What parenting habits did you learn from them?

20

20

20

## December 24
How will you celebrate the New Year?

20

20

20

## December 25

What do you enjoy most about the Christmas season or the holiday season in general?

**20** _____

**20** _____

**20** _____

## December 26

What day from this past year stands out most for you? Write about that day.

20___

20___

20___

## December 27

What daily habit does your child(ren) have that you'd like to see them keep up over the next year?

20

20

20

## December 28

What's something funny that happened recently that illustrates the way you mother?

20

20

20

## December 29
Are there any ways you'd like to get more involved with your child(ren)'s school or extracurricular life? How will you make that happen?

20 _____

20 _____

20 _____

## December 30
What famous family does yours most resemble? It can be from a TV show, a book, a movie, the news, or anywhere else.

20 _____

20 _____

20 _____

## December 31

What are your child(ren)'s aspirations? Whether it is their future career, attending a summer camp, or developing a talent, what excites them? How do you help them learn more about their interests and motivate them to believe in their capabilities? Do you encourage them to dream big?

20 ___

20 ___

20

CPSIA information can be obtained
at www.ICGtesting.com
Printed in the USA
LVHW071749290821
696359LV00004B/4

9 781638 7865